TRUCKS

Tony Potter

Illustrated by

Robin Lawrie

For Ben and Jamie

Collins

Contents

Potter, Tony
Trucks.
1. Commercial vehicles. Operation
I. Title II. Lawrie, Robin
629.28'44

ISBN 0-00-190032-3

William Collins Sons & Co Ltd
London · Glasgow · Sydney · Auckland
Toronto · Johannesburg

First Published in Great Britain 1989
© William Collins Sons & Co Ltd 1989

Printed and bound in Singapore

Under the cab

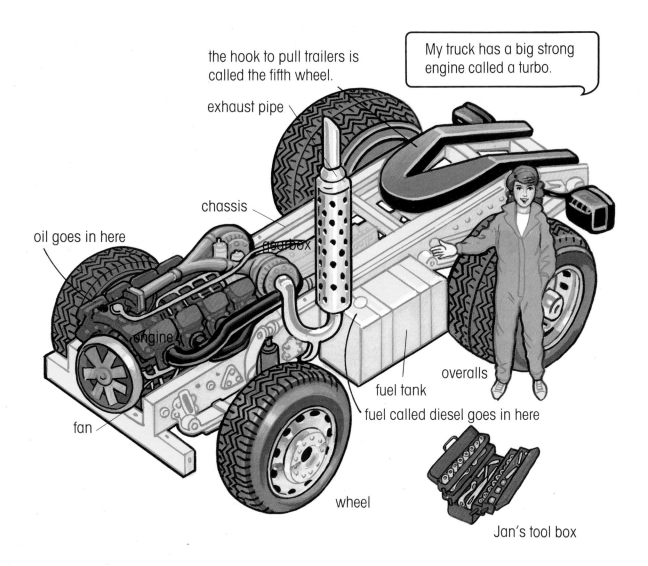

the hook to pull trailers is called the fifth wheel.

My truck has a big strong engine called a turbo.

exhaust pipe

chassis

oil goes in here

gearbox

engine

fan

fuel tank

fuel called diesel goes in here

overalls

wheel

Jan's tool box

The truck's engine and gearbox are under the cab

Lots of trucks

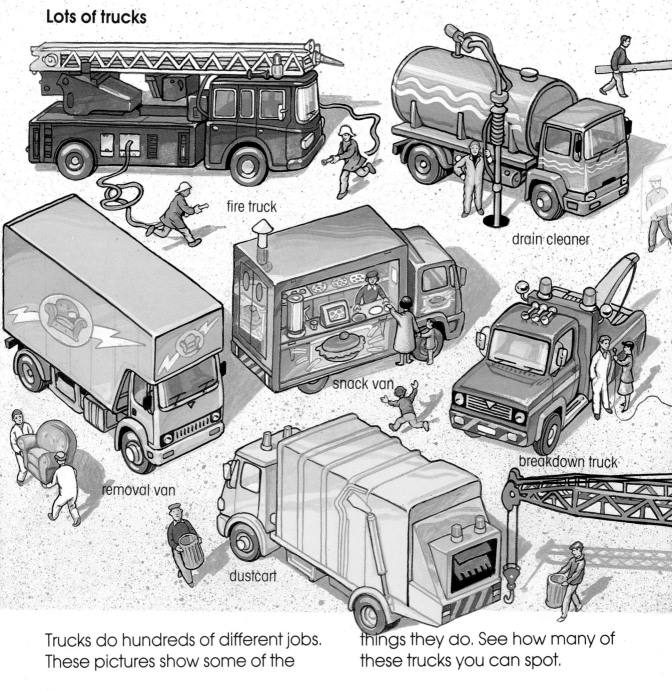

fire truck

drain cleaner

removal van

snack van

breakdown truck

dustcart

Trucks do hundreds of different jobs. These pictures show some of the things they do. See how many of these trucks you can spot.

window truck

American truck

TV station truck

petrol tanker

low loader

mobile crane

skip truck

9

Different sorts of trucks

artics bend just behind the driver's cab.

another trailer is being loaded.

I can tow different trailers with my tractor.

There are two sorts of trucks. Jan's has a tractor at the front and a trailer behind. It is called an articulated truck, or artic for short.

a fridge on top blows cold air into the trailer to keep the ice cream cold.

Jan's truck is different to Dan's. The cab and trailer are all one piece.

This sort is called a rigid truck. Trucks like this carry all kinds of loads.

Heavy trucks

Fred's concrete mixer weighs
the same as five big elephants.

Some trucks are called heavy trucks.
They are very strong and have lots of
wheels.

The tyres are often in pairs. Each pair
of tyres counts as one wheel. Try
counting the wheels on trucks you see.

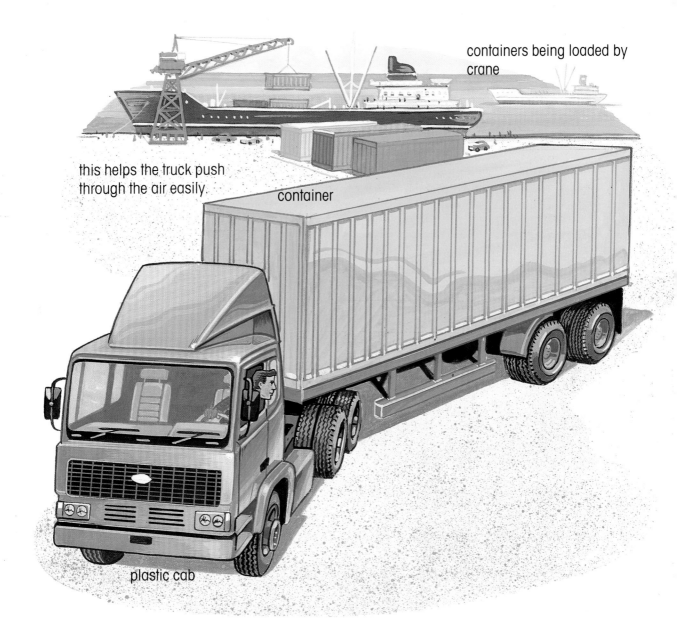

containers being loaded by crane

this helps the truck push through the air easily.

container

plastic cab

Heavy trucks need lots of wheels to spread their weight. They might damage the road if they had less wheels. Some of them have plastic cabs. They are lighter than metal cabs.

13

Medium trucks

special grab to pick up bricks.

Ben's truck

Lucy's truck

Medium trucks are not as big and strong as heavy trucks. They are used for light loads or special jobs.

Ben and Lucy both drive the same sort of truck. Ben's truck picks up bricks. Lucy delivers vegetables in her truck.

14

Dick's truck

Mac's truck

These kinds of trucks are good for deliveries in busy towns and cities. Some of them have to stop and start many times every day.

Dick delivers sand to building sites in his tipper. Mac takes bottles of drink to cafes in his truck.

15

Giant trucks

Giant trucks like this are used to build roads or work on huge construction sites.

see how small this heavy truck
looks besides the giant truck.

Loading

There are lots of ways to load and unload a truck. This digger is loading earth into the back of a tipper truck with a huge scoop

Sid is unloading a washing machine from his truck. He has a special lift at the back of the truck which goes up and down.

Breakdowns

Sometimes things go wrong and trucks break down. Drivers often fix the truck themselves.

The cab tips up on some trucks so that the driver can get at the engine easily.

this is called a winch

breakdown truck

Sometimes it is too difficult to fix a truck on the spot.

A big breakdown truck takes the dustcart away to a garage to be mended.

21

Truck words

articulated truck: a truck with a tractor unit joined to a trailer.

cab: the part of a truck where the driver sits.

diesel: a special fuel for trucks like petrol.

engine: the engine makes the gearbox go, then the gearbox makes the truck go.

fifth wheel: a special hook for trailers at the back of a tractor unit.

gearbox: the part of a truck which makes the engine's power turn the wheels.

heavy truck: big strong trucks with lots of wheels are called heavy trucks.

medium truck: these are used for light loads or special jobs.

rigid truck: a truck with the cab and trailer all in one place.

tractor unit: the front part of an articulated truck.

trailer: the part of a truck which carries the load.

this is an American road truck.

Index